DRAWING FIRE:

A COMBAT ARTIST AT WAR

PACIFIC
EUROPE
KOREA
INDOCHINA
VIETNAM

HOWARD BRODIE

FOREWORD BY WALTER CRONKITE

PORTOLÁ PRESS
Los Altos, California

© 1996 by Howard Brodie

Library of Congress Cataloging-in-Publication Data
Brodie, Howard.
     Drawing fire : a combat artist at war : the Pacific Europe Korea
Indochina Vietnam / Howard Brodie : foreword by Walter Cronkite.
       p.   cm.
    ISBN 0-9641932-1-3 (pbk.)
    1. war in art. 2. Brodie Howard. 3. Artists – United States –
– Biography. I. Title.
NC 139.B75A2 1996
741' .092 – dc20
[B]   95 – 33748
                                                       CIP

Printed in Hong Kong
By C&C Offset Printing Ltd.

Photograph of Howard Brodie on page 158 ©Renee Lynn
Design and Layout by Bruce Estes
Proofread by Angel Kao
Photographic Lab Work by Mike Lykins

Portolá Press
PO Box 911
Los Altos, CA 94023

DEDICATED TO THE SOLDIER,
FRIEND AND FOE, THEN AND NOW

FOREWORD BY WALTER CRONKITE

Despite the best that the finest war correspondent could do, it took the poet to capture the depth of a soldier's emotion. And despite the best the finest combat photographer could do, it took the artist to capture the mood of war and those who waged it.

Edward R. Murrow's epic radio broadcasts from London during the German air blitz are an everlasting part of the history of this tragic century. So too are the television images of American soldiers in battle in Vietnam.

We are familiar with the famous photographs that need no amplification – Joe Rosenthal's raising of the flag atop Mount Suribachi during the savage battle for Iwo Jima, or Robert Capa's photos of troops storming ashore during the first hours of the Normandy invasion, or David Douglas Duncan's shots of a desperate holding action in Korea and early air and ground operations in Vietnam.

The photographs are memorable as are the great broadcasts and television images from the front, but it is rare that the camera and the microphone have captured the intensely personal and overwhelming human drama caught by Howard Brodie in his drawings of American soldiers in combat.

Television and still cameras are limited by available light, by lens speed and focal length; and radio by its confinement to the hearing sense. Brodie's choice of medium is limited only by his imagination.

I first became aware of Howard's work during the Second World War where I was serving in Europe as a United Press reporter. We all read *Yank*, the Army weekly, with its *Life* magazine format of pictures and features. I remember pausing over these strangely compelling images of our soldiers in action, drawn at the very front where Howard had joined advance elements.

In the wars that followed – Korea, Indochina, Vietnam – Howard was there, in the foxholes with the troops, and his drawings were informing us, and with their unrestrained honesty, occasionally disturbing us, as they appeared from time to time across the Associated Press wire and in the weekly feature magazine – *Collier's*.

I am proud that during the early days of our involvement in Vietnam, we married Howard's artistry with the newest communications medium and brought him aboard at CBS where we showed his graphic reports on the Evening News and other telecasts.

During the famous trials of the sixties and seventies – of Sirhan Sirhan, Charles Manson, My Lai, the Chicago Seven, Watergate – Howard's courtroom scenes were a regular part of the CBS Evening News.

Howard's drawings have a great news value with their honesty and powerful spirit of urgency and spontaneity. They also leave an enduring, even haunting, impression that stays in my mind. His drawings, like all great art, direct a penetrating light onto human activity – in this case of that most ridiculous, tragic and heroic of all human conflicts – war.

I once wrote that Howard Brodie was the ultimate journalist. **I still believe that.**

LIST OF DRAWINGS

BATTLEFIELD DIARY

by
Howard Brodie

"Jump-Off" – Europe, 1944

With the Ninth Army – I joined K Company, 3rd Battalion, 406th Regiment, 102nd Division, the night before the shove-off, as an artist and not an infantryman. We were part of a reserve regiment several miles behind the line and would not be committed until after Roer [river] had been crossed by forward elements.

I felt everyone of us sweated it out as we went to sleep that night. At 0245 our barrage awoke us but we stayed in our sacks until 0400. After hot chow we saddled our packs and headed for an assembly area in a wrecked town about five miles away. It was a silent company of men spaced on either side of the road – the traditional soldier picture of silhouettes against the crimson flashes of shells bursting on the enemy lines in the distance.

In the assembly town, we waited in the shattered rooms of a crumbling building. It was not pleasant waiting because a dead cow stank in an adjoining room. We shoved off at daylight and came to gutted Rurdorf. I remember passing crucifixes and a porcelain chamber pot on the rubble laden road and pussy willows as we came to the river. A pool of blood splotched the side of the road. We crossed the Roer on a pontoon bridge and moved on. The forward elements were still ahead of us a few miles.

We passed a still dogface on the side of the road with no hands; his misshapen, ooze-filled mittens lay a few feet from him. Knots of prisoners walked by us with their hands behind their heads. One group contained medics. In their knee-length white sacks, emblazoned with red crosses, they resembled crusaders. In another group were a couple of German females, one of them in uniform. Mines like cabbages lay on either side of the road.

We entered the town of Tetz and set up the CP [command post] in a cellar. Two platoons went forward a few hundred yards to high ground overlooking the town and dug in. We were holding the right flank of the offensive finger. Several enemy shells burst in the town. Some tracers shot across the road between the CP and the dug-in platoons. The tracers seemed to be below knee level. Night fell.

The CP picked up reports like a magnet: "The Jerries are counterattacking up the road with 40 Tiger tanks . . . The Jerries are attacking with four medium tanks." Stragglers reported in from forward companies. One stark-faced squad leader had lost most of his squad. The wounded were outside, the dead to the left of our platoon holes. It was raining. I went to sleep.

The next day I went to our forward platoons. I saw a dogface bailing his hole out with his canteen cup . . . saw our planes dive-bomb Jerry in the distance . . . saw our time-fire burst on Jerry, and white phosphorus and magenta smoke bombs. I saw platoon leader Lt. Joe Lane playing football with a cabbage. I saw a dead GI in his foxhole slumped in his last living position – the hole was too deep and too narrow to allow his body to settle. A partially smoked cigarette lay inches from his mouth, and a dollar-sized circle of blood on the earth offered the only evidence of violent death.

Night fell and I stayed in the platoon CP hole. We didn't stay long because word came through that we would move up to the town of Hottorf, the forward position of the offensive finger, preparatory to jumping off at 0910.

K Company lined up in the starlit night – the CO, the first platoon, MGs [machine guns], third platoon, heavy weapons, headquarters and the second platoon in the rear – about 10 paces between the men and 50 paces between the platoons. The sky overhead was pierced by thousands of tracers and AA bursts as Jerry planes flew over. Again it was a silent company.

At Hottorf we separated into various crumbling buildings to await H-hour. We had five objectives, the farthest about 2 1/4 miles away. All were single houses but two, which were towns of two or three houses. We were the assault company of the Third Battalion.

H-hour was approaching. A shell burst outside the window, stinging a couple of men and ringing our ears. We huddled on the floor.

It was time to move now. The first platoon went out on the street followed by the MGs and the third platoon and the rest of us. We passed through dogfaces in houses on either side of the street. They wisecracked and cheered us on. We came to the edge of town and onto a broad rolling field. The third and first platoons fanned out in front of us. Headquarters group stayed in the center.

I followed in the footsteps of Pfc. Joe Esz, the platoon runner. He had an aluminum light case upon which I could easily focus the corner of my eye to keep my position and still be free to observe. Also, I felt if I followed in his footsteps I would not have to look down on the ground for mines. He turned to me and commented on how beautifully the company was moving, properly fanned and well spaced.

Several hundred yards away I noticed Jerries running out of a gun position waving a white flag. A black puff of smoke a few hundred yards to my right caught my attention, then another closer. I saw some men fall on the right flank. The black puffs crept in. There were whistles and cracks in the air and a barrage of 88s [German 88mm field gun] burst around us, spaced like the black squares of a checkerboard surrounding the reds. I heard the zing of shrapnel as I hugged the earth. We slithered into the enemy 88 position from which I had seen the prisoners run. Somebody threw a grenade into the dugout.

We moved on. Some prisoners and a couple of old women ran out onto the field from a house. Objective One. There was the zoom and crack of 88s again. A rabbit raced wildly away to the left. We went down. I saw a burst land on the running Jerries. One old woman went down on her knees in death, in an attitude as though she were picking flowers.

A dud landed three feet in front of T/Sgt. Jim McCauley, the platoon sergeant, spraying him with dirt. Another dud ricocheted over Pfc. Wes Maulden, the 300 radio operator. I looked to the right flank and saw a man floating in the air amidst the black smoke of an exploding mine. He just disappeared in front of the squad leader, S/Sgt. Elwin Miller. A piece of flesh sloshed by Sgt. Fred Wilson's face. Some men didn't get up. We went on. A couple vomited. A piece of shrapnel cut a dogface's throat as neatly as Jack the Ripper might have done it.

The right flank was getting some small-arms fire. I was so tired from running and going down that it seemed as though my sartorius muscles would not function. The 300 radio wouldn't work and we couldn't get fire on those 88s. Pfc. George Linton went back through that barrage to get another one from Hottorf. Medic Oliver Poythress was working on wounded in that barrage.

Objective Two loomed ahead – a large building enclosing a courtyard. A cow shed, stables, tool shed, hay loft, and living quarters opened on the inner court. I saw an 88 explode over the arched entrance.

We filtered into the courtyard and into the surrounding rooms. The executive officer started to reorganize the company. The platoons came in. 1st Sgt. Dick Wardlow tried to make a casualty list. Many didn't make it. A plan of defense was decided on for the building. A large work horse broke out from his stable and lumbered crazily around the courtyard. T-4 Melvin Freidel, the FO [forward observer] radio operator, lay in the courtyard relaying artillery orders. An 88 crashed into the roof. The cows in their shed pulled on their ropes. One kicked a sheep walking around in a state of confusion.

A dying GI lay in the tool room; his face was a leathery yellow. A wounded GI lay with him. Another wounded dogface lay on his belly in the cow shed in the stench of dung and decaying beets. Another GI quietly said he could take no more. A couple of doggies started frying eggs in the kitchen. I went into the tool shed to the dying doggie. "He's cold, he's dead," said Sgt. Charles Turpen, the MG squad leader. I took off my glove and felt his head but my hand was so cold he felt warm. The medic came and said he was dead.

Lt. Bob Clark organized his company and set up defense. FO Phillip Dick climbed the rafters of the hay loft to report our artillery bursts. The wounded doggie in the cow shed sobbed for more morphine. Four of us helped carry him to a bed in another room. He was belly down and pleaded for someone to hold him by the groin as we carried him: "I can't stand it. Press them up, it'll give me support." A pool of blood lay under him.

I went to the cow shed to take a nervous leak. A shell hit, shaking the roof. I ducked down and found I was seeking shelter with two calves. I crossed the courtyard to the grain shed where about 60 doggies were huddled.

Tank fire came in. I looked up and saw MG tracers rip through the brick walls. A tank shell hit the wall and the roof. A brick landed on the head of the boy next to me. We couldn't see for the cloud of choking dust. Two doggies had their arms around each other; one was sobbing. More MG tracers ripped through the wall, and another shell. I squeezed between several bags of grain. Doggies completely disappeared in a hay pile.

We got out of there and our tanks joined us. I followed a tank, stepping in its treads. The next two objectives were taken by platoons on my right and I don't remember whether any 88s came in for this next quarter mile or not. One doggie was too exhausted to make it.

We were moving up to our final objective now – a very large building, also enclosing a courtyard, in a small town. Jerry planes were overhead but for some reason did not strafe. Our tanks spewed the town with fire and led the way. Black bursts from Jerry time-fire exploded over our heads this time. We passed Jerry trenches and a barbed-wire barrier.

Lieutenant Lane raced to a trench. A Jerry pulled a cord, setting off a circle of mines around him, but he was only sprayed with mud. S/Sgt. Eugene Flanagan shot at the Jerry, who jumped up and surrendered with two others.

Jerries streamed out of the large house. Women came out too. An 88 and mortars came in. I watched Pfc. Bob de Valk and Pfc. Ted Sanchez bring out prisoners from the basement, with Pfc. Ernie Gonzalez helping. An 88 crashed into the roof and a platoon leader's face dripped blood, but it was a surface wound. Jerries pulled out their wounded on an old bed spring and a chair.

We made a CP in the cellar. The wounded were brought down. Stray Jerries were rounded up and brought to the rear. Jittery doggies relaxed for a moment on the beds in the basement. Pfc. Frank Pasek forgot he had a round in his BAR and frayed our nerves by letting one go into the ceiling. A pretty Jerry girl with no shoes on came through the basement. Doggies were sitting down now. The CO started to prepare a defense for a counterattack. Platoons went out to dig in. L and M Companies came up to sustain part of our gains.

Most of us were too tired to do much. The battalion CO sent word he was relieving us. All of us sweated out going back over the field, although this time we would go back a sheltered way. We were relieved and uneventfully returned to a small town. The doggies went out into the rain on the outskirts and dug in. A few 88s came into the town and some time-fire near the holes. Early the next morning, K Company returned to its former position in the big house with the courtyard at the final objective. Just when I left, Jerry started counterattacking with four tanks and a company of infantry.

ASSAULT ON A HILL – KOREA, 1951

It is dark before dawn. Strings of little cans of blue heat flicker dully in the gloom like votive candles in a dimly lit church. G Company, 2nd Battalion, of the 7th Regiment of the 3rd Division is heating C-rations for breakfast on a knoll before jumping off for Objective 11. "You'll be lucky if you only run into 100 Chinese on that hill. . . Watch out for booby traps and they have pack howitzers," I remember these words from a briefing in battalion CP last night.

Three tanks rumble up to join us. "Saddle up," snarls the exec. We amble down to a road and line up on the shoulders. "Aw right, move out, pass it along." We walk on, black silhouettes against a brightening sky: third platoon, second platoon, weapons with first trailing. Bandoleers, some in garlands of four, drape from necks. Field jackets bulge from stuffings of C-rations. A bayonet flaps, hooked to the center of the back of a GI's web belt. "He likes it goosy," quips a dogface. We approach a wooded hillock, the line of departure. It's a foothill to higher 11. It's daylight now. "Keep that five yard interval, damn it, now many times do I hafta tell ya?"

We dip down from the hillock and move up to the phase line on a shrub-covered lower ridge of our objective. The crack of artillery bursts rips the silence. Black smoke blossoms of our preparation cluster around the crest. Five minutes pass . . . ten. We're waiting for the white blossom. The phosphorus shell signaling the end of our barrage. Capt. Hugh Casey goes into a huddle with his platoon leaders. He assigns platoons to center, left and right flanks. A croaky-voiced Tennessean sings about hard work and an easy woman. "Shut up, you wanna sock on the snot-locker?" snaps a tense dogface. The white burst looks like cotton. The platoons fade out into the foliage. Our mortars thump. Their bursts "walk-up" ahead of the platoons. A few minutes pass. Then, rat-tat-tat-burp! we hear the sharp, crackling sounds of a firefight.

We move quickly down into a gully and up the eroded, forward side which forms a natural barrier against the enemy. Captain Casey goes forward. Cpl. Edward Reynolds, the 300 radio operator, and I join him. Weapons platoon remains behind. The antenna sticks above the scrub pines like the feeler of a big bug. We step down a drop and up a bank. Suddenly, the phing-humm! of bullets. We drop and slither into the brush. Whn-n-hmn! Pine cones drop. "Jesus," says Reynolds. He spreads his thumb and index finger indicating the closeness of one. Battalion tries to communicate with us on the 300. "Halo Able, this is Killer Six, Over . . .Halo Able, this is Killer . . ." "Tell 'em we're pinned down," says the captain.

Up ahead there are whistles, rebel yells, cuss words. GIs are making a charge. Only my ears form the picture. We are in a world within a world, pinned down. The shouting subsides, but not the staccato sounds of shots. A half-hour passes. It seems I know each root, rock and pine cone in my microcosm. Then voices to our left. Through the branches we see GIs plodding down. Some help others. "Who's that?" shouts Casey. "Second platoon," gasps a dogface. "Rosy 'n' O'Malley 'n' Morgan are still up there. God! . . . Rosy's dead." They slog down and disappear into the eroded gully. We stoop-shoulder back, scoot over a rise and drop into the gully with them.

Sniper bullets whine across the top. A skirmish line is formed. We stoop, creep and crawl in the clefts of the little arroyo. It looks like a posse's stand in a Western movie. Red-bearded Marion Gray sets up his machine gun and fires. "I see 'em up in that clearing to the left," pants a GI. M1s crackle on the firing line. A dogface turns and says to me, "I'm fighting for ma's apple pie." Machine gunners slither to new spots. It's SOP to change position each time they fire. Medics work on wounded lower in the gully. "What a birthday present: I'm 18 today," says Luther Arnold, lying on a stretcher. His gift is shrapnel. There is a red stain on the crotch of one wounded GI's fatigues. A GI puffs a cigar; another reads a comic book. Some relieve themselves. A GI in front of me leaps into the air as a spent bullet buzzes by him. Hot cartridges pop from weapons. Dogfaces open C-rations. Sebastian Madrigal opens a can of tamales and pulls a bottle of chili sauce out of his pocket. "Two wounded comin' in; pass it along," is relayed down the bank. Hulking John O'Malley breaks through the foliage carrying Stanley Rosenberg of Brooklyn in his massive, Rodin hands. Blond whiskered Cloyde Morgan follows. They brought Stanley back. A mortarman rushes up to Rosenberg and shouts, "I thought you was dead, Rosy, I thought you was dead." He kneels, grips Rosy and kisses him. Rifleman Morgan turns his head away. He is crying.

The second platoon moves out. Captain Casey and the command group go with it. We move quickly and low. The platoon fans out ahead of us. "Creep and crawl; pass it along." echoes an order. We elbow up a knoll, move onto a shrub-covered hogsback. The phing-hmn! of the sniper. We lie head to toe up the hogsback like prostrate worshippers. The sole of a combatboot of a GI is inches from my nose. I watch his hamstring muscles quiver. His body recedes in grotesque perspective.

We're on a sub-peak now, below the objective. We make contact with the third, and weapons platoon comes up from behind. The first is ahead, screened from us by foliage, assaulting the crest. Bullets rip into the flesh of a sergeant in the first platoon. He scrambles for cover and sits. A bullet pierces his neck. He slumps forward, dead. On a left flank slope a GI prays, "Lord if you'll get me outa this one, I'll stick up for you forever."

The second and third fan out. The command group moves up behind the sweeping infantrymen. The enemy is fleeing from the crest beyond us. We are upon the first holes. Though I am a couple of feet from them, they are difficult to see in the brush. "Throw a grenade in 'em, sweep 'em clean," commands an officer. There's a dead enemy. "He didn't give up," says a dogface, lobbing a grenade into his hole. "Yup, gave up his ghost," retorts a GI firing his weapon into an adjoining position.

On the crest an enemy throws concussion grenades. A GI shoots him between the shoulder blades. The enemy turns and moves his lips. A bullet blasts his mouth. An infantryman sinks his bayonet into a foe's flesh. Another crashes his rifle onto the skull.

We move up. The brush is honeycombed with holes. There's an acrid smell in the growth, like burned fireworks on the Fourth of July. We pass a pitfall in the center of the trail. We reach the crest. Dogfaces are silhouetted against a darkening sky. Objective 11 is secure. A machine gun fires at the fleeing enemy. Fox Company files up to relieve us. There's a voice on the 300 radio, "Halo Able, this is Killer Six, Over." Captain Casey picks up the phone, "Killer Six, this is Halo Able, Over." "Halo Able, you can bring your chickens home now." "Roger and out."

Guerrilla War – Vietnam, 1965

I walked to war from Da Nang with two American advisors and a native Regional Forces platoon. At the edge of town crowded buses rolled on the road and pedestrians padded on the shoulders.

We filed onto a paddy path to a hamlet. And, searched family dwellings and a temple. Sweatsplotched soldiers squatted. Children played. Women cooked. We chowed, wrapping crepes around a paste of peanuts, eggs, greens, then, dipping them with chopsticks in Nuoc Mam sauce, the drippings of pressed pungent fish.

A trooper holding papers rushed from a hootch with a teen-aged girl. "VC documents!" the platoon circled the pair. One Yank advisor snarled, "She's a VC, SHOOT HER!"

"You're not going to!" I groaned.

"Take her away and SHOOT HER!"

"FOR CHRIST'S SAKE, NO!"

The mother rushed to her daughter's side. The trooper ordered them taken to the rear, under guard. I followed.

At the press camp, I talked about the deathly drama around a bar table. "I saw a VC executed in the field," said a journalist. "He was shot in the legs first, then, upwards."

Coca Colas fizzed in our frosty glasses.

A cameraman showed me prints of bound VC in a row on their knees, being shot in the nape of the neck by a native trooper.

"Where were the American advisors?" – I sensed my advisor's order was unusual – "Wouldn't someone protest?"

"Wouldn't do any good. Vietnamese feel our bombing and napalming of women and children are worse."

"That's not DELIBERATE killing of the helpless!"

"Well, sometimes Charlies have been executed because they can't be guarded – don't forget the VC have mutilated and killed."

Sampans slipped by on the river.

A witness to a South Vietnamese interrogation of a VC spoke, "I saw them pull down his pants, attach electrical wires to his testicles and shock them 'til he talked, then they blew out his brains."

An American officer sighed, "My troops strung up a VC. We prodded him with charges, then cajoled him with cigarettes – I feel it's justified if the information we get saves our men's lives."

Choppers beat overhead.

"Men have been brutal in all wars," commented a correspondent.

"THE HELL THEY HAVE!" I fired. "Not in World War II and Korea – maybe some in isolated cases."

"This is a GUERRILLA WAR! Anyone can be dangerous: boys, girls, elders. What are you trying to do, bring MORALITY into WAR?"

I headed to the chopper base passing a sign posted in front of the chaplain's tent: If you think it's hot here Wait 'til the hereafter.

Crews readied a squadron to evacuate peasants terrorized by the VC from Khre Tre. Boarding one of the 18 transports, I saw our escort gunships rake the ridges as we touched down in the valley. A stream of humans, 1,654 fathers, mothers, babies, youths and elders flowed toward us bearing their belongings leaving their homes and crops. Their silence, sighs, and cries saddened the lonely land.

Back in camp, I joined dusty journalists. Sex reports were savored. One whored on nights before going into the field, others after returning. Fear seemed forgotten with focus on fornication.

A GI on a mission forced a mother to her knees for fellatio but was stopped by his officer who later slaughtered the villagers. Natives hawked "Fuck Books" to grunts. A larger-than-life clear plastic vagina adorned an officers' club. War seemed an aphrodisiac.

Green flares sizzled on the perimeter ridges. Artillery boomed and geckos chirped as I slipped under my net and sacked out.

Rising early, I climbed aboard a Caribou enroute to a Special Forces A-Camp. Green Berets were rugged, resourceful select troops involved in overt, covert, civil, and military actions – a waggish one handed me his calling card:

Tigers tamed, Assassinations plotted,
Revolutions started, Opium dens opened,
Bars emptied, Orgies organized

Nosing down between jungle peaks, the trim transport shuddered to a stop at Gia Vuc. I jumped into the "suicide seat" next to the Special Forces driver of the truck. Nungs – Chinese mercenary bodyguards – rode in back. As the vehicle rumbled on a narrow road, the Beret jammed on the brakes. Three imbedded pointed logs surrounded by panji sticks jutted toward us! "VC ROAD BLOCK!" Our bursts CRACKLED. Silence, wrenched by CRIES. A moaning old man and two wailing women bore a bleeding young man to us. He died.

The Caribou carried me back to Da Nang. I boarded an Otter for Hue. Two young American women in civilian dress boarded. "We're Wycliffe Bible translators," smiled an attractive girl. Bouncing over ridges ribboned by waterfalls, the courier touched down in Kae Song. I gazed at the girls departing to bring knowledge to tribes in Quang Tri province amidst war.

Lifting again, the Otter banked in sight of the Laotian jungle hiding the Ho Chi Minh Trail, then, spiraled sickeningly down, snaked feet above elephant grass, and shudderingly stopped on the strip of Aloui.

Berets guided me through barbed-wire barriers, past a mine field, a muddy moat studded with panjis, through sand-bagged slotted walls, into the old French fort manned by native irregulars and Nungs.

"Ask the cowboy, if you need anything," I was told in the team bunker. "Cowboys are Saigon delinquents serving their sentences working for our forces."

CRACK! CRACK! CRACK! reverberated. "VC shots" shouted the shaggy-haired cowboy. I barreled out behind the Berets. Nungs calmly gestured the direction of incoming rounds. "They only tense with VC mortars," shrugged a sergeant.

Sliding into our bunker sacks, we pulled blankets up in the cool mountain air. Rats pattered along our logged roof. One spiraled down by my side. "Sorry 'bout that," soothed a Beret. Several times I had been moved by this sensitive remark, until I realized this was the Nam version of "Tell it to the chaplain" in World War II to cool complaints.

Morning. A C-123 escorted by fighters circled the valley. Our walkie-talkie crackled with word from above. "We're getting fire!" The fort's 105 field piece BOOMED. The round burst on a VC ridge. I moved to the strip with a platoon of departing Nungs – one lit incense strips tied to his rifle barrel for good luck. The transport streaked down. Nungs with a squealing pig and I clambered into its belly. The "Shuddering Shit House" ROARED down the runway, cleared trees and climbed.

Wet with sweat at camp, I jeeped with correspondents to China Beach. After plunging into the surf, we savored pineapples, peeled and spitted like giant lollipops by peddling boys. And, saw the white bodies of grunts, their heads and arms browned, redden under the burning sun on R and R.

I headed to the CP of a Marine battalion. The CO pointed to the floor of his tent. "My sergeant killed a poisonous snake." Moving forward, I sketched a gaunt grunt whose buddy had been killed a few feet away. Boarding an amtrack, I dropped through the hatchway into the steamy hold with sweaty grunts. The tractor churned downriver. The ramp opened. Leathernecks swept a village. Natives eyed us peacefully. Circumcised kids splashed in the song. Pulling back to a rise in lonely paddy fields, grunts manned foxholes wary of any sound or sight during the night. The morning sun shone on approaching figures – women hawking warm bottles of Coca Cola!

A squad moved out on patrol. Lead leathernecks disappeared in elephant grass. Through the overhead blades a temple appeared. "The patrol got ambushed there yesterday," breathed a grunt. "We burned three gooks, they got one of us." We moved through the house of worship on the blood-stained floor and, circled back.

I bounced to battalion on a truck. The driver swerved to smash a snake. The big one slithered off a shoulder.

Pulling up at the motor pool, I entered the sergeant's tent THIRSTY. Uncovering wet sacks over a cooling hole, he lifted a flagon from his buried treasure and poured me a cup. Savoring each swallow as it coursed through my body, I MARVELED at the WONDER of CLEAR COLD WATER!

Darkness dropped. CRACK! CRACK! CRACK! Gunfire on the perimeter. "VC PROBE!" The sergeant and I jumped into his foxhole. Slowly he pointed. On the rim, a BIG BLACK COIL! We stiffened with snake fear. A flare flashed. The ominous coil – a tow rope!

Sunup. I moved to the Thu Bon Song past ghostly dwellings and paddies without peasants. "We moved them all out," said a grunt. "The area's cleared."

Sundown. Five men slipped out from the perimeter. Crickets screeched, bats squeaked. One grunt slithered up a mound with his walkie-talkie. Another kneeled, peering into surrounding shadows, a third sacked out with his grenade launcher, the fourth balancing his rifle on his chest, snored. The kneeling watch jabbed, "Snorin' can be dangerous." Turning on his side still balancing his rifle, the snorer wheezed, "It's my pacifier."

Watches changed. I eyed the new grunt on the mound – VC had wiped out four dozing

LP [listening post] teams. The beat of sticks. "VC drums!" The grenadier pressed his .45 into my hand. I pressed it back – he had offered me a grunt's greatest gift, his only defensive weapon. My heart warmed.

After sunup, a couple of grunts sneaked off to the song for a swim. CRACK! CRACK! VC sniper. Litter bearers bore back a bather. A corpsman administered morphine.

A grunt broke through the brush chasing a chicken for chow. After chow, a squad filed out on patrol. Sweat splotched our fatigues, oozed under our bullet-proof vests. We glanced down for patterns of twigs or green leaves – which don't fall from foliage – marking VC mines.

Taking five in a deserted dwelling, we jerked up. Across a paddy, a native padded. "Dung Lai!" shouted leathernecks. He didn't halt. "Dung Lai!" yelled the leader. "Fire warning shots!" Tracers arched over his cone hat. Still, he moved on. "FIRE ON TARGET!" Tracers streaked toward him, ricocheting off the path. The Vietnamese went down. A grunt with a pocket bible shook his head. The native slid from sight behind the paddy path.

"We'll get out of here!" barked the leader.

"You're not going to leave him," I groaned.

"Might be a trap, MOVE OUT!"

My spirit shrunk each step away. The native gnawed at my guts returning to the perimeter. I stretched out on my sack saddened and silent as a human likely lay dying behind a bank while sunset shadows lengthened into night.

Moonlight. Another patrol. "Be careful of spider holes," whispered the leader on the path, "some have panjis." Hearing strange sounds, he pointed to a cluster of trees. Moving ahead with the point, he returned with propaganda leaflets. "Maybe the sounds were a lure."

Following the point at several foot intervals, we filed on a paddy path guarded in the rear by "Tail End Charlie." "Halt!" sounded his voice, CRACK, his .45. His speedy steps slapped the path alongside us. "A gook was on the path behind me!"

CRACK! CRACK! CRACK! VC fire from the paddy. Tail End dropped for cover. The grunt ahead roll-dived. The one behind tossed a grenade into the paddy. BOOM!

Silence. We drawled, crouched, ran. I fell into a spider hole, held my breath, no panjis, breathed. My helmet clanked down the path. Clambering out, I scrambled to the squad taking cover at a thicket edge.

Hostile bursts CRACKLED from trees. We slithered, flattened. My heart trip-hammered. Bullets WHINED overhead.

The leader whispered in the radio, "Delta 6, Alpha 31, Victor Charlie, " Alpha 31, pull back."

Whitened with tension, we pulled back over the blued terrain to the perimeter, where I glanced at the red, white and blue propaganda leaflets:

U.S. COLORED ARMYMEN!
You are committing the same ignominious crimes in South Vietnam that the K.K.K. clique is perpetrating against your family at home. . . .

Sunup. A grunt spilled a sack of artful carvings on the soil. "I'll send 'em home; we're gonna burn the hootches anyway."

Boarding an amtrack, I headed back. The tractor grated to a stop beside a squad with a VC. I sketched the PW bleeding from an ear, his ankles tied, wrists bound behind. A grunt reaching down for his wrist ropes from the high deck yanked up the wrenched, dangling, grimacing human. At battalion, I mixed with peasants relocated from the field circling the CO. His sergeant sidled up to me. "One of our short artillery rounds killed a relative but we'll pay the family a fee."

Returning to Da Nang, I boarded a C-123. The transport shuddered as it climbed, shaking its cargo of troops: the lively gabbing about leaves, the leaden slumping in sleep, the lifeless swaying in plastic bags. Troops jumped out at Tan Son Nhut. KIAs were trucked to the base mortuary. Soldiers on the shoulders spontaneously saluted their bagged brothers.

Riding into Saigon, I checked into the Caravelle Hotel. Elevators lifted with grimy-fatigued, muddy-booted correspondents coming from combat, lowered with safari-suited, shiny-shoed journalists heading to battle briefings.

Dropping my gear, I shook hands with my roommate, a photographer. We chatted about our wives and children. He headed out on assignment. I showered wearing my gamy fatigues, stripped under the warm water, then, shivered stepping out in my air-conditioned room. I slept in a sweater.

But, sweat in the morning joining a company of the 173rd Airborne Brigade saddling packs for a search and destroy mission in War Zone D.

"It's all Charlie Company," said a trooper. "We're gonna destroy everything, even dogs."

"Not me," groaned a buddy, "I like dogs."

"VC eat 'em."

We streaked our faces with green and blackish grease paint, attached leaves to our helmets, and boarded trucks. The half-tons rumbled to Ben Hoa. Jumping down, we formed in fives and climbed into choppers of the first wave.

Our slick lifted. Thumbs up to buddies below. Space rapidly filled with the strike force. Troopers dangling legs from decks bantered across the void with comrades on close choppers. Then, silenced as escort gunships CRACKLED, their tracers streaking into the jungle, rockets spiraling: BOOM, BOOM, BOOM. Bursts blazed from side guns on slicks – an incoming shot bloodily nicked a pilot.

Our chopper shuddered descending with side gunners raking the jungle. Troopers and I leapt off. "SPREAD OUT!" yelled the leader firing into rotor-wind-lashed brush. A VC mortar round burst. Another. We joined squads firing into foliage.

The jungle stilled. Not the sky. The second wave of slicks CHOPPED down. Fresh troopers poured through our positions forming a perimeter. We joined them at sunset.

Moonlight pierced the jungle canopy blueing the faces of white troopers and blending black buddies into the bush.

A squad slipped through the perimeter to set up a VC ambush. I grabbed the pack strap of a black to find my way in the file of Negro troopers, a sole white behind. We stealthily snaked our way in silence on a footpath. The sergeant hushed, "Halt," positioned troopers and a MG in brush, and motioned me to stay with the white below a large-leafed tree.

The trooper spreading his poncho, signaled me to throw mine over his. We slipped between the rain gear like sweaty meat in a rubber sandwich. The squad stilled.

The RUSH of rain. Our tree became a leaky umbrella. Drips spattered on the poncho. Drops beat on the big flat leaves overhead. Why no whispers? Minutes moved to hours. A snore from my sackmate. I tightened. And snores from the brush along the path – I, an artist with pencils, the only one awake for the ambush! A squishy sound on the path! My lungs locked. Another squish closer! My skin prickled. Another sucking sound! Should I awaken my buddy to kill? Or let VC kill us?

KILLING! – the agony that had gripped me since World War II: GIs had dropped amidst 88 bursts. Zinging shrapnel had slit a doggie's throat. Another had floated amidst the black smoke of an exploding mine. A hunk of flesh had sloshed by a sergeant.

Another sloppy sound! A plop near by boots! I wildly stared upwards. A big leaf unfolded pouring its pool to plump on the path – THE FOOTSTEPS!

Breathing heavily 'til sunup, I rejoined company and panted, filing forward. At times, I saw only the trooper ahead and behind as we wove through the jungle. "Take five," was relayed back. I sat spent spreading my legs on the path and angling my arms back in the brush. A sergeant eyed me. "Don't move, snake!" He unsheathed his knife. "It's a Five Steps!" And cut off its head. "You take five steps and drop dead!"

Energized with fear, I lightly stepped forward. Clouds covered the sun. Lightening flashed. Thunder CLAPPED. Rain poured. Upturning our helmets, we gulped sweaty water. The sun shone. Our fatigues steamed.

We slogged past a sizeable dugout bedded with grass. A bloody blanket, open cans of fish lay about – a VC field hospital. "You can tell Charlie just left." A trooper pointed: "The bugs haven't eaten the fish."

Settling in sparse jungle, troopers burned leeches off buddies' bare backs with glowing cigarette butts leaving bloody suck spots. Setting charges on trees, they blasted a chopper clearing.

Climbing into a chopper, I flew back to Ben Hoa. Jeeping to Saigon, I saw a tracer streak across the four-lane American-built highway – three thousand troops flown on one hundred and twenty choppers into a hostile zone had searched for, but not found, enemy to destroy. Yet, Viet Cong harrassed the freeway to the capital!

My assignment was completed. I'd head home. But not the young father who shared my room – he was killed in action.

PACIFIC & EUROPE

1. Physical Examination

I walked in the line of naked men at induction center, taking the physical examination: "Open your mouth . . . jump up and down . . . Take a deep breath–hold it . . . Clench your fist . . . Ever wet your bed? . . . Read the last line . . . Spread your cheeks apart . . . Ever have scarlet fever, heart trouble, mumps? . . . Cough . . . Do you like girls?

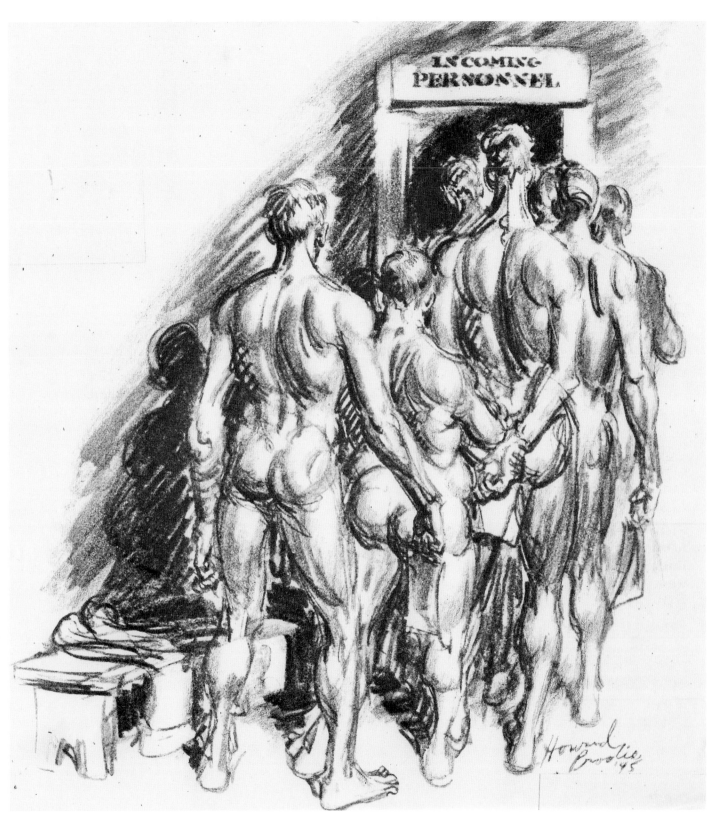

2. Road to Kokumbura, Guadalcanal, During Advance

A body was on the shoulder of the road, partially mashed by the traffic of the fast push. I became aware of another by a sickeningly sweet smell after we had passed over him. I glanced behind the jeep and saw a "pancake" man so flattened and dust covered he appeared part of the roadbed. I walked back from Kokumbura and followed the smells to the swollen bodies in the brush near the road. After sketching a few, I no longer felt the need to see any more.

3. Matanakau River

Going up the Matanakau River with GIs, I helped push and pull the boat over the shallows. We passed a lizard about three feet long. Coming around a bend, when I felt we might be dangerously close to the enemy, we passed under a clothesline of GI laundry stretched across the stream. I disembarked at an aid station where wounded were loaded on the boat for the return trip. I hiked up to the Horse's Neck front, where GIs fired into the jungle from a lower ridge. Three carried back a Jap prisoner on a shelter half. During the night, I watched an attack by "Washing Machine Charlie" [Japanese bomber with unsynchronized engines] on our units near the beach.

4. Flying Fortress Mission

I went on a bombing mission in a Flying Fortress named "Sad Sack." Rising from the tropical heat to the cold of high altitudes necessitated wearing warm gear and oxygen masks – warm beer was sometimes placed aboard to be chilled when the plane landed. The bombardier was stripped in the heat of Henderson Field.

5. Squad Leader

After a siege of malaria, I was ordered back to duty in the U.S. and then sent to Europe. In Germany I met S/Sgt. Elwin Miller as his company was preparing to attack. There was a MG bullet in his helmet from previous action, for which he received the Purple Heart, Silver Star and British Military Medal.

6. Moving Up

I moved up with GIs. It was a silent company of men, spaced out either side of the road. I remember passing crucifixes on the rubble-laden road . . . and pussy willows as we came to the river.

Sgt.
Howard Brodie '45
Europe

7. Taking a Break

During a break while moving up, a GI rested his pack on a fence post.

8. Forward Observer

I went into an upstairs room of a shelled farmhouse with this FO. A mortar round burst outside and a piece of shattered glass stung him. Many homes had crucifixes.

9. Nature Call

I slept in a CP in a stonewalled basement of a farmhouse. Several mortar rounds burst outside during the night. Next morning I had to relieve myself in the open. It was then I realized the tension of a GI on the line performing this simple, necessary act.

Sgt. Howard Bivchë '45
Germany.

31

10. Winter

I made this conception of GIs in Winter, after field trips had made me realize how numbing the cold was.

Sgt. Howard
Brodie '45

33

11. Flare!

Returning from B Company – 1st Battalion, 116th Regiment, 29th Division – which could not be reached in daylight, I followed two GIs down a snowy, mortar-scarred road at night. Suddenly we were caught in a flare! They froze in their positions. One kept his arm outstretched – they knew if they moved they might be detected, but motionless, they might appear part of the landscape.

12. Street Scene

During one of the long lulls, GIs moved a sofa down a street to make their quarters comfortable. I heard a platoon leader say to his men, "Treat those feather beds carefully, this is somebody's home and they're coming back."

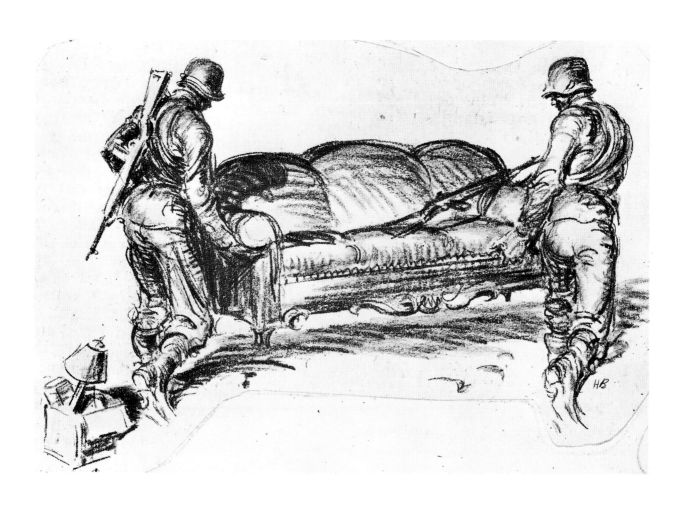

13. Moving up with K Company

3rd Battalion, 406th Regiment, 102nd Division – we passed a still GI on the side of the road, with no hands.

52.

CAPTION ON REVERSE SIDE.

14. Platoon Runner Joe Esz

After K Company jumped off near Hottorf, Germany, I followed in the footsteps of Pfc. Joe Esz. Platoons were advancing ahead of us. Joe and I took cover for a minute behind a haystack. Ahead was the final objective. He said "You know, I could never kill a man. I aim over their heads and hope they surrender."

To Melvin Friedel
with best wishes

Sgt.
Howard Brodie '45
Germany

41

15. Going for Cover

Infantrymen went down for cover often in an 88 barrage.

16. Exploding Mine

I saw a man floating amidst the black smoke of an exploding mine on the right flank. Later, I made this drawing, adding details, since I had seen him from a distance.

17. 88 Dud

During an 88 barrage a dud landed in front of a platoon sergeant, spraying him with dirt. Another ricocheted over the 300 radio operator and one landed behind a medic.

Sgt.
Howard
Brodie '45
Germany

47

18. Medic

The medic behind whom a dud landed was Oliver Poythress who worked on wounded in the barrage.

19. Head Wound

During the attack I saw a GI run by, holding his head wound.

20. Compassion

K Company GIs reached a farm and huddled on a grain shed: Tank fire came in now. I looked up and saw MG tracers rip through the brick walls. A tank shell hit the wall and the roof. A brick landed on the head of the boy next to me. We couldn't see for the cloud of choking dust. A man held another sobbing in his arms.

21. Dead GI

On a front line I saw a dead GI in his foxhole, slumped in his last living position – the hole was too deep and narrow to allow his body to settle. A partially smoked cigarette lay inches from his mouth, and a dollar-sized circle of blood on the earth offered the only evidence of violent death.

Sgt. Howard
Brodie '45
Germany

22. Malmédy

I illustrated the massacre at Malmédy from accounts of survivors: "The outfit was put into one group and a German officer searched us for wrist watches and took our gloves and cigarettes . . . We were marched into an open field about 100 feet from the road where German tanks were moving by. There were about 150 of us, counting officers and medics. We all stood there with our hands up when a German officer in a command vehicle shot a medical officer and one enlisted man . . . Then the MGs on the tanks opened up on the group . . . ."

23. Execution

I watched the execution of three German soldiers who had been posing as GIs by an MP firing squad during the Battle of the Bulge. It was December 23rd, 1944, morning and cold. They were dressed only in fatigues painted with vertical prisoner stripes. Their hands and ankles were tied to posts. Knees slightly sagged on the outside men; the center soldier stood erect. He protested having his eyes covered, but all were blindfolded. White target circles were pinned over their hearts. An Army chaplain spoke to each . . . stepped back. Shots thudded into the closest man's chest. He slumped forward, knees buckled, blood spewed from his mouth.

Sgt. Howard Brodie
'45
Germany

24. V.J. Day

This was my conception for war's end.

KOREA

25. Troop Transport

On board U.S.S. Bayfield with Marines bound for Inchon and Wonsan.

26. Drying Socks at 27° below Zero

One morning it was 27° below at daybreak. . . Our shoe packs crunched into the hard snow.
Mucus froze under the noses of the men. I pulled out my canteen but had to chip the ice from
the neck before I could drink the water.

27. G.I. on Guard

I sketched this G.I. standing guard atop his sandbagged foxhole in a courtyard on the 1st Cavalry Division front.

PVT.
FRED
M.
GIBSON
HARRISONBURG
VIRGINIA
ON GUARD
AT CO. CP
1ST CAV.

28. Captain Forrest Walker

I joined an Easy Company attack on Hill 233 commanded by Captain Forrest Walker. Over his shoulder he advised me, "You better stay with the weapons platoon; they'll be in the middle." We jumped off: second platoon in the lead; weapons platoon behind it; first bringing up the rear.

"Where is the third platoon?" I asked.

"There is no third," answered a GI. "We've had too many casualties."

"YEA, THOUGH I WALK THROUGH THE VALLEY OF THE SHADOW OF DEATH"

29. "Dancing to the Burp-gun Boogie"

Just as Hill 233 came into view, there was a sharp burst of fire and the file flew apart as we scrambled for cover. There was silence. "Let's go!" shouted the lieutenant. A mortarman "carrying" the carbine of his buddy, leaped. His buddy carried the mortar tube.

Korea

H Brodie
'51
To my friend, Ed
Cunningham — always
the best Howard

30. Sergeant James White

Once again automatic weapons started up. Sergeant James White of Alabama jumped up, planted his legs firmly, and roared, "Dammit, MOVE!" We moved.

"DAMN IT, MOVE, YOU BASTARDS"

SECT. SGT.
JAMES WHITE
BREWTON ALA

31. From the Crest of Hill 233

Ahead, isolated squads of the lead platoon fought their way to the summit under small-arms fire. Silhouetted were the figures of several GIs, their rifles aimed down the other side.

32. Bringing back the Dead

Two days before a platoon had been shot up on the hill and the body of its leader still lay on a slope. I looked up. A little group of men moved down Hill 233, four GIs bearing the body of the platoon leader.

33. Jigai

On the 2nd Division front near Yongsan I saw three figures crossing a rice paddy: A GI carrying a wounded South Korean buddy on a jigai [a native carrier] with a rifleman guarding the two. Blood dripped from the wounded man's mouth onto the GI's helmet. Quickly the medics went into action. The wound was examined. Morphine injected. He was placed on a litter jeep.

34. "Cracker Box" Ambulance

A stream of casualties poured into the CP: glassy-eyed battle-fatigue cases, shrapnel-torn bodies and the waxen faces of shock. A company medic was brought in . . . he died. A litter jeep arrived with a tiny bundle, a baby found behind a rock. I squeezed into a "cracker-box." A GI held his head in his hand. "Water, water," gasped a supine figure. A combat-fatigue case stared and tensed his hands into claws. Someone vomited. Moans accompanied bumps as the ambulance rumbled to the rear.

35. Marion Gray

I saw this machine gunner on a skirmish line while on attack on Objective 11 with G Company. Sniper bullets whine across the top. We stoop, creep, and crawl in the clefts of the little arroyo. Red-bearded Marion Gray sets up his MG and fires. Later he was killed in action.

DOGFACE
PFC MARION D. GRAY
BROWNSVILLE PENN. E.R.

36. 300 Radio Operator pinned down by cross-fire. Cp. Edward Reynolds, G Co. – 2 Bn., 7 Rgt. – 3rd Div.

. . . the antenna sticks above the scrub pines like like the feeler of a big bug. Suddenly, the phing-humm! of bullets. We drop and slither into the brush. . . pine cones drop. . . Reynolds spreads his thumb and index finger indicating the closeness of one.

radio operator under sniper
fire — missed him by
inches

37. "I thought you was dead, Rosy"

Hulking John O'Malley breaks through the foliage, carrying Stanley Rosenberg . . . Blond-whiskered Cloyde Morgan follows. They brought Stanley back. A mortarman shouts, "I thought you was dead, Rosy, I thought you was dead." He kneels, grips Rosy and kisses him.

"I thought you was dead, Rosy."

38. Rifleman Morgan Weeps

Watching the mortarman embrace his wounded buddy, Morgan turns his head away. He is crying. I may have been the only one who noticed Morgan wipe tears from his eyes.

39. War Refugees

To get to Seoul I had thumbed a jeep ride from Taegu: on a dusty mountain road we passed a long file of refugees. Among them a man carried an aged woman on a jigai roped to his back. In the rubble of Waegwan I had to thumb again. Thousands of refugees poured through the city – like ants in a line that vanished over the horizon.

93

VIETNAM

40. Portrait: French Foreign Legionnaire

I was with the French in Indochina many years before the Vietnam War sketching Foreign Legionnaires from Hanoi to the Chinese border. This corporal chief posed for me in his chapeau brousse – German seemed the common language of enlisted men: many Wehrmacht men, including SS, joined the Legion after their defeat in the Second World War. I heard them singing the Horst Wessel song.

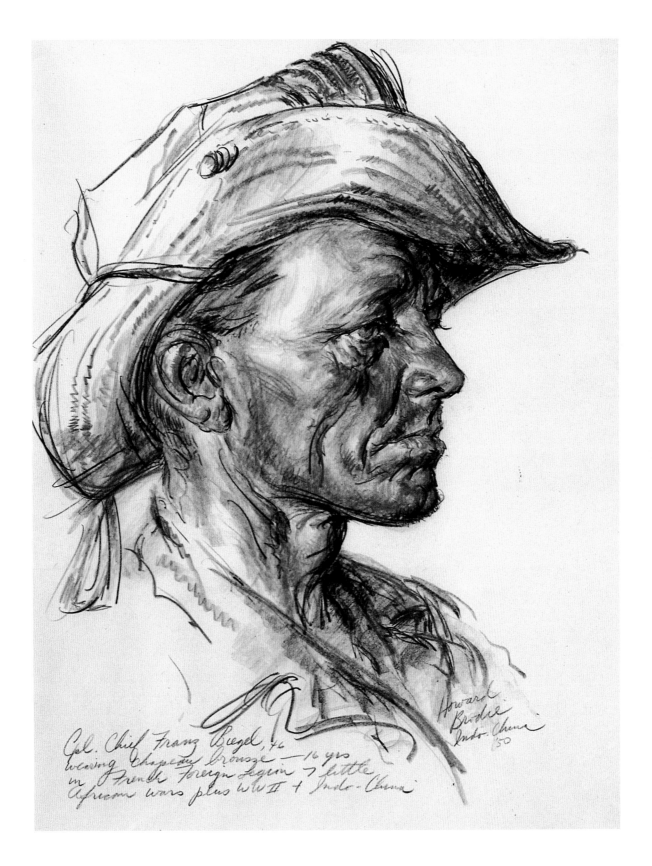

Col. Chief Franz Biegel, 46
wearing chapeau brousse — 16 yrs
in French Foreign Legion 7 little
African wars plus WW II + Indo-China

Howard
Brodie
Indo-China
'50

97

41. Saigon Traffic

Horns HONKED. Jeeps, trucks, bicycles, pedicabs, motorscooters, motorcycles, motorcycle-cabs, and horsedrawn carts rolled on the rues. GIs, Green Berets, Airmen, Sailors, Marines walked on ways with Aussies in slouch hats, Yank construction workers in safety helmets, pilots with shoulder holsters, native troops in tiger and leopard fatigues, and graceful women in pastel au dais.

42. Youth Group

Youths posed eagerly. One pimped, "You wanna numbah one girl?" Others shined shoes.
Thunder roared, rains poured. Kids flopped in the gurgling waters.

Shoe Shine Boys

Howard
Brodie
'66
Saigon

43.   Sketch: MP Behind Drums

44. Sketch: Guard Behind Sand-bags

Buildings were guarded behind concrete-filled steel drums and sand-bagged posts.

33rd Air Base Squadron TAN SON NHUT 2nd Air Div
Security & Law Enf. Sect.

Told me how all airmen stand at attention here
spontaneously when a flag-draped casket in station wagon
passes by en route home.

Air Policeman in sand bagged sentry post.

H. Brodie 65
Saigon

45. Portrait: Fighter Pilot

At Tan Son Nhut airport, I sketched a fighter pilot. "I felt terrible after my first mission," he breathed. "The village didn't seem like a military target – but we warn natives who are not VC to get out beforehand by loudspeaker and leaflet." Super Sabre jets ROARED off on missions.

Fighter
Pilot

107

46. Portrait: Native Trooper

I walked to war with a native platoon and two American advisors. In a hamlet children played, women cooked. VC documents were found in a hutch. An advisor ordered the resident, a teen-age girl, to be shot! I PROTESTED. She was brought back under guard.

NGUYEN VAN TY
12ᵗʰ COMPANY
NG APO 4563
NG VAN TY

DAI DOI 12
DAI DOI 12
KBC 4563

C 4563

Binh
Vietnam
65

South
Vietnamese
Airborne
trooper — fought
at Dien Ben Phu
for French

47. Sketch: Pilot in Flak Vest and Diapers

HOLES IN
PLANE

VH-34D
TRANSPORT
HELICOPTER
PILOT

IM
FLAK
VEST
+
FLAK
DIAPERS

Berdin
65
Viet Nam

MARINE
CAPT
ROGER
FETTERLY
PESHTIGO
WIS

111

48. Sketch: Pilot in Vest

Heading to a chopper base, I sketched pilots in flak vests and diapers – VC bullets could pierce bottoms of choppers and crews.

Marine

1ST LT.
WARREN
"PETE"
PETERSEN

PENSACOLA
FLORIDA
or
STOUGHTON
MASS

HELICOPTER
-34 PILOT

18 holes
IN PLANE

purple
3 dead

MISSED
AGAIN
RATFINK

VC BULLET THROUGH FRONT
AROUND SIDE & OUT BACK OF
HELMET... MINOR GLASS CUTS

113

49. Portrait: Crew Chief

A chopper crew chief groused, "KIAs are the worst to bring back. They can be stiff, in awkward positions, and can stink – a medic gave me a vial of ammonia so I won't pass out."

Howard Brodie
Vietnam '65

MARINE
CPL PAUL BANKI, CREW CHIEF OF A UH-34D
MILWAUKEE WIS TRANSPORT HELICOPTER

50. Portrait: Airborne Soldier

An airborne soldier posed for me moments before he took off on a mission. "He looks like a Masai warrior," said a buddy.

JAMES TATE SGT
BOGALUSA
LOUISIANA
CO A
2nd Bn
503
173
BDE
APO SF
96250

Airborne
paratrooper
sketched
waiting
to take
off on
Brigade
attack

Howard
Brodie
65
Vietnam

117

51. Pilot in Huey

I boarded a "Huey," a UH-1B attack helicopter. Waist and shoulder straps fastened pilot in place. Burp guns hung from bucket seats. Lifting off, the shuddering "gunship" fostered the feeling of flying with noisy wings on an angel of death.

INSIDE
UH-1B
"HUEY"
ATTACK
HELICOPTER

TRACERS

ARMY
WARRANT OFFICER
CLAYTON
WRIGHT

MOLINE
ILLINOIS

52. Door Gunner

Door gunners with cinched belly bands gripped smoke grenades with pulled pins to toss the red markers on VC positions, and fired their MGs. Bursts flashed muzzles. Tracers streaked into the jungle. Hot cartridges popped into the cabin. The gunship JOLTED, as our sizzling rockets spiraled forward and BURST!

UH-1B
"HUEY"
armed, attack
Army
helicopter
gunner

53. Troopers Leaping

"Slicks" touched down. Troopers leapt off, into rotor-wind-lashed growth. A VC mortar round burst. Another.

54. Trooper Pointing

"Spread Out!" shouted a squad leader, then fired into the foliage.

"Spread out"

Impression of Cpl. Jimmie Long ordering his team on attack

55. Squad in Elephant Grass

Our squad wove through elephant grass wary of VC and snakes.

56. Sergeant

The sergeant eyed me as I sat spent, spread – my legs forward and resting back on my angled arms. "Don't move, SNAKE!" He unsheathed his knife. "It's a Five Steps."   And cut off its head. "You take five steps and drop dead."

Buchu
Viet nam

He killed
snake on
operation,
identified it
as Krait
("5 STEPS"
called here)
5 steps +
you drop
dead

129

57. Alternate Fire Positions

The squad took alternate fire positions. "We burned three gooks yesterday," whispered the leader, "they got one of us."

U.S. Marines
alternating fire
positions during
pause on patrol

PFC RICHARD
DORAH, ST.
PETERSBURG FLORIDA

LANCE CPL
RONALD HEFLEY, NORTH CHICAGO

Berdie
65
Vietnam

58. Listening Post

Darkness dropped. The squad formed a listening post. Crickets screeched, bats squeaked, sticks beat. "VC drums," whispered the watch. The grenadier pressed his .45 into my hand. I pressed it back – didn't carry a weapon. He had offered me a grunt's greatest gift, his only protective weapon. My heart warmed.

59. Watch

The sleepy watch dropped his head, JERKED it up – VC had wiped out four dozing LP teams.

135

60. Sketch: Roll-dive

VC FIRE! the grunt ahead of me roll-dived.

Brodie
'66
Vaet   Incoming fire grunt roll during in
ditch

61   Sketch: Fall into Spider Hole

"Be careful of spider holes," whispered the leader, "some have panjis."   One fell into a spider hole. Another tossed a grenade.

Falling into
panji hole
marine night patrol

62. Troopers Flattening, Slithering

Bullets WHINED overhead. We slithered, flattened. Hearts trip-hammered. The leader whispered "VICTOR CHARLIE" on the radio. "Pull back," crackled from the CP.

63. Litter Bearers

A grunt sneaked off to a song for a swim. CRACK! CRACK! VC sniper! Litter bearers brought back the bather. A corpsman administered morphine.

Howard Brodie
'66
Vietnam

wounded on front
South of Da Nang
He had gone swimming & sniper got him

64. VC Prisoner

Grunts captured a VC. I sketched the PW bleeding from an ear, his ankles tied, wrists bound behind.

145

65. Grunt Chasing Chicken

A grunt chased a chicken for chow.

Grunt scrounging chow on front near Da Nang
(sniper fire in area)

66. Grunt Bathing Kids

A leatherneck with a bucket splash-bathed delighted kids at a well.

Marine Cpl Barry Tatom, Detroit, Mich
"I like kids"

"People to People"

Splash bath @ combat outpost near village

H Bertie 65
Vietnam
near DaNang

67. Body Bags

Returning to Da Nang, I boarded a C-123. The transport shuddered as it climbed, shaking its cargo of troops: the lively gabbing about leaves, the leaden slumping in sleep, the lifeless swaying in plastic bags. KIAs were trucked to the base mortuary at Tan Son Nhut. Soldiers on the shoulders spontaneously saluted their bagged brothers.

68. PBR Gunner: Night

Heading to the Mekong River, I boarded a PBR [U.S. Navy river patrol boat] for a night patrol. Gunners were alert for VC on banks in the dark, and for forbidden cargo on sampans at daybreak.

The River Patrol Boats
on Mekong Vietnam

69. PBR Gunner: Day

River patrol boat gunners eyed the foliaged banks of the Mekong for VC on the dangerous waters during the day.

Broke '66 Vietnam

River Patrol
Gunner

SM   LARRY BIGLER   16 CITY AVE. LANCASTER S.C 700 pdo

70. Peasant Portrait

The haunting eyes of a peasant stayed with me as I completed my assignment in Saigon. I could head home, but not my roommate – he was killed in action.

ABOUT THE AUTHOR

Born in 1915 in Oakland, California, Howard Brodie was educated in San Francisco schools: Polytechnic High School – alma mater to many famous athletes and statesmen – and then the California School of Fine Arts, the oldest art school in the West. His first job as a professional was on the *San Francisco Examiner* as a photo-retoucher. After a year or so on the *Examiner*, Howard moved over to the *San Francisco Chronicle* as a full-time sports illustrator.

Following Pearl Harbor Howard found himself at war, signing on as a combat artist for *Yank Magazine*, the Army weekly. Sent first to Guadalcanal, he eventually covered many of the major campaigns of the Second World War including the Battle of the Bulge. For aiding the wounded and for coolness under fire during the battle, Sergeant Howard Brodie was awarded the Bronze Star.

It was on Guadalcanal that he turned to the use of a kind of wax pencil sold under the brand name of Prismacolor. Having run out of his regular drawing pencils, Howard discovered that the U. S. Navy was using Prismacolor pencils for marking on map overlays. "Borrowing" some of the Navy's pencils for his immediate needs, Howard found them so satisfactory that he continued to use them throughout the war. They worked in Korea at 27° below zero while wearing gloves, and in Indochina and Vietnam under rainforest conditions and triple canopy jungle cover. Prismacolor pencils were used for all of drawings reproduced in this book.

Howard Brodie lives with his artist–wife, Isabel, on a ranch near Parkfield in central California.